Dusk at Pimlico: Short Stories on everything from Love, to the Self, Childhood, Culture and London.

By Julian Kasey Jan

The creative process can be an isolating one. This was a solo project in its entirety. I wrote, edited, and formatted this book by myself, I apologize if I am sloppy but I am an independent author and this gave me control, and freedom of my work. Something everything creative wants and should have.

Foreword

This book of short stories was written upon my return to my native Britain in September of 2017. Although I have visited Britain, mostly London, a dozen times since I left in 2000 and moved back to the United States (I also lived in several other countries since, including: South Korea, Japan, Turkey, Pakistan, and Qatar). I then moved back twice to Britain, however, they both became long visits, rather than any type of permanent settlement. The first attempted return home was to London (I lived in Bayswater, a central part of London, just near Hyde Park in 2004). I came to study Law at my Alma Mater, The University of Westminster, but a financial dispute between myself and my father cut my stay very short. I lived in Bayswater for just three months.

My second return to Britain to live was in 2007. I returned after working for my cousin Umar (on my father's side), who exported cars to Africa. He had made an attempt to establish a business in the Dominican Republic. Like most business ventures, it was a risk, and it became an isolated and turbulent one for me, as a personality conflict developed between myself, and a local named Pablo (who was also working for my cousin). Being the businessman my cousin was, he sided with Pablo, who clearly had the upper hand in business affairs on the island. Umar gave up his business ventures in the Dominican after a couple of years anyway. I left the Dominican after just eight months and went back to my home town of Huddersfield, West Yorkshire. I took a National Express bus there from Heathrow airport. Although, there was family support in Yorkshire, the job market was a difficult one. With two master degrees earned, the only job prospect that I could find was as a door-to-door salesmen. So I started to look for jobs teaching English on the serious teacher's website. I found one in Istanbul and left Yorkshire after just two months.

Now in the year 2017 on this return home, no one greeted me when I arrived at Heathrow airport. I had two suitcases, one full of clothes and the other full of my most prized possessions--my books. I had no place to live. So I had to do a flat search. I left my bag full of books at Heathrow left luggage. Then I took the Heathrow express train to my old neighborhood of Paddington in central London and stayed at the Park Grand Hotel for a couple of days. After two nights, I moved to the Henry VIII hotel, also in Paddington. During my first week in London, I must have spoken with a dozen Estate Agents and looked at a studio flat in St. Johns Wood and a two bedroom in Hampstead, but prices were very high and flats (apartments) very small.

In June and July of the previous summer I visited Scotland, and started my trip in Edinburgh, then went to Inverness, the Isle of Sky, and Glasgow. I found The Scots to be a warm-hearted people and many strangers took me "emotionally in." I was so moved that I thought I might relinquish my London roots and make my home in Scotland. After staying five nights at the Henry VIII, I checked out and spent one night at The European hotel so I could be near Kings Cross Railway station. I took a train from London Kings Cross to Edinburgh. The next day I ended up staying in Edinburgh for a fortnight (two weeks). I stayed in two hotels while I was there: the Toby Carvery In the town of Christorphine, and the Leonard Hotel in the Haymarket area, close to the centre of Edinburgh. I found it difficult to make my home there and struggled, despite continuing to meet nice people and make new friends. I never connected with the two friends that lived there, because I was perpetually flat hunting. There is an application system in Edinburgh to obtain a flat and this was a busy time of the year, as Edinburgh has several universities and many students flat hunting. I ended up looking at seven flats and many of them there had four of five students also looking; and many desperate to take the first flat then saw. What also did not help my flat search, despite a warm-hearted staff at the Toby Carvery, there was the limited access to print off applications. I had to ask the staff behind the bar, so by the time I printed off many of the applications the flats were already gone. Even the short term letting market was difficult. I found an agency that let for only let short term lets and I liked several ones that were sent to me via email, but when I asked if I could view those of interest, I would get back "unfortunately that flat has been taken." This went on for several emails, and by the fourth email I had given up. I replied, "Unfortunately due to not finding something I am leaving Edinburgh." .

Then my wife and son who were supposed to move back to the UK would not be joining me. So I started a search for short term flats in London online. I saw one in Pimlico, an area in central London in the borough of Westminster. I really liked it, mainly because of the scenic and picturesque view. On Friday October 18, I gave the agency that was letting the flat Hamptons a ring, and asked if I could take the flat over the phone. The polite estate agent said,

"Sir we usually don't do that, it's better to arrange a viewing first."

I had purchased an advance ticket on the train planning to head back down to London on November 4, but I told the agent I would come down to London on Monday October 21 for a viewing, so out the window the train ticket went on the 4th. I went down to London on Sunday. I even was supposed to check out of the Leonard hotel on Monday so out the window one night went too. I returned to London, stayed in the Duke of Leister in Paddington. The seventh hotel I stayed since moving back. I had a look at the flat on Monday and I told the agent that I don't need to look at anything else, and would take it. She just stared at me, moved slightly side to side anxiously nervous, and said "ok." We left the flat and as soon as we got out of the building, she was on the phone calling to speak to the landlord. The process started that day and contracts were signed after a couple of days. I moved in 5 days later on Friday October 26.

The building is called The Panoramic, it is just before Vauxhall Bridge and the building has been in a television series and a film. The 1970's television series the Sweeny and the film Skyfall, a recent James Bond movie.

These are stories that I wrote during this exciting, hectic, emotional and at times a dark, isolating time; as I had no job and no place to live and not sure when I would see my son again. The first three set of stories: love, the self and culture, I wrote in hotels while I stayed in Edinburgh; with the exception of The Battle of Gandamak, which I wrote at a Nepalese restaurant there. The remaining set of stories childhood and London I wrote in my flat at the Panoramic.

However turbulent a time it was, I had a sense of relief and gratitude to be back in Britain and the city of London. Which of all cities in the world I have lived in, this is the one I would truly call home. Due to moving here in 1994, in a subconscious way I had come back to my youth.

There is a tone of anonymity throughout the book, as I came across people I met on this journey who were friendly and kind, but some who were also suffering, just like I did, and like we all do at times in our lives. I hope you enjoy my stories.

Dedicated to all people of the City of London, England.

One: Love

The Only Woman in the World

I remember the way you looked straight into my eyes, I could see just the pupils of your deep blue eyes on the dance floor. You were so in control, focused: your stern countenance was gone; you had that subtle smile I saw on your face, you knew exactly what you wanted and how to get it. You were so in control, focused, confident. The snap of your fingers, and that slight tussle of your body; when the music stopped, and just before the next song, you gulped your wine as if you were in a hurry to increase your desire, but you kept your smile subtle, as your gazed now heighted into my eyes. Yet you kept dancing, you were the woman in control. As a young man that once moved all over the dance floor so confidently with no inhibitions or cares in the world, I have aged and just moved side to side like a shy little boy. When the dancing was over, we were going home together. Once back home the shy boy became a confident man once again. I made love to you so slow and easy like time was endless and there was nobody else in the world but you and I.

Two: The Self

The Prisoner

Early Morning. My wife is already up and I hear her in the family room crunching on some cereal. I don't want to get up but I want to see how she is doing. We chat a little bit and then she gets ready for work. She then is dressed and ready to go. I kiss her goodbye. This was the slowest year of my business but I resorted to other active methods to keep me busy. I worked on my autobiography, went to the gym, read. I talked to hardly anyone except workers on my compound, on my morning walks and just a greeting, "Good Morning," "Good Morning Sir," But none of them would call me by first or last name. And in this age of social media and cell phones, I only get messages and texts. I rarely talk to friends and family. At times just like a prisoner that has to ask for permission to make phone calls to some of them, at times I have to do the same. My evenings are empty and dull, I stare at four walls, and then at a box that is supposed to be a form of entertainment and information. Alone again in solitary confinement. Just like a prisoner. I read before I go to bed, lay my head down to sleep but then I awake up at 3:30am. I lay there sometimes until 5am. Dear God, when will I break free of this cycle, set me free. I am innocent, not guilty but I am the prisoner.

The prisoner, Part Two

I wake at 3:30am, sometimes 5:30am. I cook myself some food, read a newspaper, then I might go back to bed when at any time I want to. The rest in the afternoon stops the butterflies from going through my head. I bathe when I want to. I check my emails, even social media. Anyone but my lawyer I do not ask permission to call them because I won't. I am in solitary confinement still but the drab view of the vacant street in my bedroom is gone. I embrace the isolation and read, write and meet street people. I was the prisoner but now have been set free.

Three: Childhood

Grandma and Grandad's house

A lay in my bed on a Saturday morning in Pimlico. Relaxed. I hear the loud but ever so subtle tick of the clock hung on my wall. It's so familiar just like the sound I used to hear when I would visit my grandma and grandfather in West Yorkshire. Up the train I would go from Kings Cross to Wakefield Westgate. Sometimes I took a taxi or the bus to their bungalow in the village of Clayton West. In the summer the door would usually be open with colored strips hanging from the door that one always puts their hands in front to pass to walk through." Has someone come?" She knew it was me and all it took was a phone call to tell her I am coming. She would get up with the biggest smile on her face that raised her cheekbones; dressed in usually very traditional dresses with big patterns on them, beige shoes, ones I remember with straps, and I remember that bright blue dress so well. I would drop my luggage in the front room, or put it in my guest room at the back. She would get things started right away." Let's put kettle on." One time I went up to visit when I was a young self-employed professional. I came dressed in a dark pin stripe suit. My grandfather felt my suit and said, "I am very proud of this young man," he even passed the news on to my other relatives later that I had come dressed in a suit.

Gran would serve four or five courses a day. Eggs and bacon for breakfast. Full course lunch, of roast beef Yorkshire pudding, vegetables and mashed potatoes with gravy. There was a wooden square table at the end of the sitting room in the bungalow. Before meals, it had to be pulled out to make it a round table. My grandmother would lay down a white and blue-checkered tablecloth that today might be considered vintage 1960s. She then would boil water and wash and dry the plates we ate from to keep them warm. White crockery ones with brown trim. Forks and knives with slightly faded wooden handles and there was also salt and pepper shakers and HP sauce put on the table, as well as bread and butter.

My grandmother would say at the table before I started to eat,

"Get weaving" (start eating). There never was too much talk at the table. My grandfather would ask me if "I am alright." The talk was saved for after the meal, and if there was any talk that became serious, my grandfather would lift his fork and knife, never pointing it at anyone; make his point in the conversation and get back to eating his meal.

After a few hours, tea and cake would always be served and then I would retire to my bed in the back room, there was a big clean washed duvet. If it were cold, my gran would put several hot water bottles in my bed. Warm, calm relaxed and so every peaceful she made me feel.

I remember a New Year's Eve I spent with them and my grandparents although both in their late seventies, they would stop up late. The clock struck midnight and as we were just sitting in the front room on the green sofa, my grandfather would be sitting in his designated armchair. It was his place where he would hold court about issues of family, politics, and his time spent as a soldier in Africa during the Second World War and memories of my mother and my auntie Jenifer, as well memories of him and my grandmother. Suddenly, when the clock struck midnight, both of them got up, and said, "Happy New Year!", and were in a very celebrative mood. My grandfather said,

"Let's do the tradition of bringing in the New Year." "What is that?" I asked. He said, "Go outside and then open the door." I did and I was greeted by both of them "Happy New Year!"

I can still see that big smile on my grandfather's face, full of joy, he turned to my grandmother and gave her a kiss. Although now I just see them in my dreams and all I hear is the sound of the ticking clock on my wall.

The Battle of Gandamak

I remember my father telling me about the battle of Battle of Gandamak. It was a battle fought in Afghanistan in the First Anglo Afghan war in 1842. Four thousand British troops went to fight in the battle but only one medical surgeon (Dr. Brydan) on a horse ever came back. Ignore your foes and friends, at times-- let them come to you.

Four: Culture

The Pub

The pub in any of the countries in the British Isles is not just a watering hole. The pub is sitting by a warm fire in winter, or to cool off with a drink in the summer. The pub is sport and football colors. The pub is where anger can take place. The pub is where conversations are made, and promises broken, love is found and love is lost. The pub is where the working class make their living. The pub is where the lodger sleeps. The pub is Sunday dinners. The pub is family. This pub in the town of Christorphine is my shelter, covering me from the Scottish brisk wind and rain. The pub is yours, whether you're young or old.

Five: London

Taken in Yet Again

London, the first time I just showed up on your doorstep was a quarter of a century ago. Just like my grandmother did with a smile and welcoming yet loving stiff upper lip, there were few questions asked. Twenty-five years ago, my abode was a pub in Islington. John the landlord asked for no references, or background check, his welcome was opening up his arm by his side with his big belly posed straight at me. An Irishmen, he hardly had a stiff upper lip, it was just him giving me the benefit of the doubt. After I moved out of the pub, I never saw him again. Now my grandmother is gone too, and I have lost touch with some of the friends I made when I moved to London twenty-five years ago. I am alone, but embrace what is left. Every day I find a new restaurant or bookshop to go to, and meet a new person to speak with. It's as if every day is an adventure. Now my emotional comfort lay in the hands of the four concierge in my penthouse high-rise building. Some of our conversations go deeper than just about the weather and I get to know each of them as individuals, it was due to them that I was taken in emotionally--yet again.

Dusk at Pimlico

The six large windows of my 20 story building in Pimlico, The Panoramic, give me a view of London that I have never seen before. With a view of a park at Beesborough Gardens in front of me and a busy street with black London cabs and bright red double decker buses. In the distance, is just a slight scatter of clouds in front of a light blue sky. The sun goes down so slow and easy just like a lazy man on a Sunday afternoon without a care in the world. The church tower is cone shaped grey brick, but with a strong tint of black that years of smog have discolored, with ever so small oval windows on the steeple of the church. It stands behind the terrace houses and looks like it could touch right to the heavens. Planes fly above amongst the clouds, one after another. I think of my son and try to reach for the heavens in some intangible way to touch him. I am dreaming. My penthouse high rise breaks the high piercing sound of the busy street, making it so minute. There is no noise of cars, buses or people, maybe a siren of an ambulance. A sound that I am ever so familiar with; it makes that "wha wha" noise. In some non-nonsensical way it comforts me. It's a familiarity of my childhood. The time I missed living in England; the mother I have missed growing up without, but this is today, and its dusk in Pimlico.

My Son Kasey

I walked past a library advertising books for children, every time I see a father with his child or toys I think of you. I picture that golden blonde hair of yours with that part in the front of your hair, that bashful grin on your face when you look at me. When your cartoons are on you used to say the morning "Daddy Daddy, sit down," and when your mum put on Mary Poppins in the evening you used to say "London London." Daddy is London now without you, but you are in my heart as you always will be. I love you.

The Grosvenor Pub

My every Monday afternoon lunches at the Grosvenor Pub on Grosvenor Road. There is not a sole in the pub but me.

You and Me

I was tired. Tired of being humiliated, treated like a child, belittled, and living in fear that my child would be taken away from me. While people religiously watch men move or hit a ball up and down a field, eat and indulge, drink, dance, fuck, don't care; people suffer. They are the physically and mentally ill, they are the man I saw asleep on the London tube early Sunday morning, sleeping, *as* stop after stop goes by, he never got off on any of them. He was going nowhere. He is someone's son, or even father, maybe even someone's husband. On this day, I went to the Imperial war museum in Lambeth North London, before I went in the museum I went and bought a coffee, and sat on a bench. Across from me, I saw a man sitting alone on another bench. He was putting his hands on his ears, but I impolitely stared. I looked at the wrinkles on his face. I looked into his eyes and I read into a life of too much pain…. That was his Sunday afternoon. There are men and women like him suffering in London. They are children, they are the old, the poor, they are veterans whom have served in the military, they are your sister and brother, your mother or father, and they are you and me.

Order, Discipline and Englishness

Every night I stare at the view of the bright white Georgian Terrace houses from the view of my penthouse. I look at each one in a row, all the same. Each has the exact same four story Victorian windows with black doors as pitch as coal. The order and design of them reminded me of what the philosopher Jeremey Bentham wrote about called the Panopticon.[1] All the terrace houses are so neatly in a row and in order. Each had the same windows, pitch-black doors, fence in front of the first floor window, with four Irons on each fence. It represents order and discipline, just like the transport policemen I saw on the tube the other day. I bid him a good afternoon but there was no reply, such a stern countenance and a stare back. He kept his guard. I went to visit the Banquet house near Westminster, the site where

---

[1] This is what Bentham wrote of how to describe the Panopticon or as he called it the inspection house, his definition. "Containing the idea of a new principle of Construction Applicable to any sort of Establishment, in which persons of any description are to be kept under inspection; and in particular to penitairy- houses, lazarettos, manufactories, hospitals, madhouses, and schools; with a plan of management adapted to the principle": Jeremy Bentham, Panopiticon.

King Charles II was executed. I passed the changing of the guard on my way there. A plethora of tourists flashed their pictures at one of the guards, but there was no expression on his face. He stood still like a statue, it's as if there could have been pouring rain falling down on him, not a slight grin, or smirk on his face. It's one of the concierge in my building after having such a personal conversation one afternoon he slipped, instead of sir he said, "Great talking to you man." Today it was back to "sir." It's the receptionist at the medical clinic when I asked your name is miss? It's as varied as the houses built many years ago from social class, table manners, clothing and dress.[2] As the second most watched country in the world with CCTV security cameras, it's that sense of social order and discipline from Georgian times to Victorian which is still a part Englishness today. It's that nuance of social order and discipline that has never left England and never will.

---

[2] For additional thought I read The Englishness of Dress edited by Breward, Conekin, and Cox. While The Jeremy Bentham book is a read for the more academic audiences, while Englishness of Dress is for both academic and the popular readers. These several contributing authors discuss, dress and the social nexus of social class to dress from pre Victorian times onwards, to some of the designs by Vivienne Westwood.

Rage in His Eyes

My appointment to view the flat was at 2:00pm, I went to have a coffee in Paddington that was just nearby. I left the coffee shop at Paddington early, I always try to be early for appointments. I went to Warwick Avenue station because really I did not know where I was going. I asked the attendant at the tube station if he knew where the street was. He walked with a hunch, and had bags under his eyes, bumps for cheeks, and wrinkles on his face. It's as if life had been hard on him. I asked him where the street I was looking for was; he got up from his seat, and went to look at the map on the wall near the exit of the station. He had a good look; he said, "No, not here must be Maida Vale." I thanked him several times for his kindness. I went to Maida Vale station. I still had no clue where I was going. I looked around, and asked a few shopkeepers. They did not either know either.

They told me to ask the Estate agents. I did so, one that had mostly Asian British working there. One of them looked diligently and told me to go several streets up, and it's on the left. I thanked him several times for his efforts. I walked past several streets, asked another person where the road is. She told me far and that I need to take a bus. I kept walking. I heard the sound of a police car, and passed a man walking; in a strong London cockney accent, he titled his head towards me and he said, "Looks like cops and robbers." I did not take much notice of him and carried on walking. I saw the street I was looking for a couple of blocks later on the left hand side of the street. Next, I saw a young blonde policewoman running and a man with no shirt on in November, wearing beige shorts, short and stocky with muscles like a cartoon character. He looked as if he might be an ex-marine. He was screaming at the top of his lungs. The female police officer ran forward to him, oddly two workmen with hard hats carried on working on the roadside right in front of the raging man. I had never seen anything like it in my life, but what I saw was the rage in his eyes. They were blood shot. And then it's as if he looked straight at me, to say "back off mate." I did. There are few men that I am afraid of, but he was very muscular. Arms the size of my legs. So much so, that I believed this man could have killed someone. I went back to Maida Vale and found a Thai restaurant and went in to regroup my nerves. I called the agency. I told them what happened on the street and that I was canceling my appointment. The very calm and cool estate agent said, "That is understandable." But what I thought of is the man in rage, he is someone's son, or brother. I hope he will get the help he needs.

Discovered

I woke up with the usual high energy on a Thursday morning but disgruntled, I had a difficult night's sleep, but it did not slow me down, I was not hungry and went downstairs to the gym in the basement of my building and walked and then ran a light pace on the treadmill. Just for twenty minutes. I had not eaten anything but after going on the treadmill, I was hungry. I went to the cupboard and grabbed a Wheatabix, crushed one in a bowl and poured some milk on it. I then washed my sheets. My wife and son are coming to visit me so I wanted to tidy up a bit. By now, it was 9:30am. Restless, I had my things to buy list so it gave me a reason to get out of the house. I needed any reason. I could not in sit in my flat in isolation. I took my bag, packed a book *Bedlam, London and its Mad,* and another one about the sixties and London. Off I went. I went to a local coffee shop in Pimlico and ordered a bagel with cream cheese and salmon, and read a bit from my book *Bedlam, London and its Mad.* I went to the bank, bought some carpet cleaner and went grocery shopping. I came back to my flat and cleaned my carpet. Yet I still had energy. I did not sit. I couldn't.

I got ready to pack up and leave the flat again and wanted to go to one of my favorite areas of London to Camden town. There is shop on Highgrove Street called the Rock Shop. I have visited it a few times and there are good used cd's and have bought some great used books about music. In some of my previous visits I bought a book called *The Dream Palace* about the famous Chelsea hotel in New York, a home to various creatives from Patti smith to Sid Vicious. I talked with the owner and then bought a book for a pound. That was all I needed to do in Camden. I started to make my way home made but when I arrived, Camden town tube station was closed, I looked for a bus to take and I saw a bus that said number 24 Hampstead Heath on it. I missed it, but another bus came first that said Chalk Farm so I hopped on it and it stopped at the Morrison's grocery store in Chalk Farm. I walked towards Chalk Farm station, and saw a big red brick building that said the Roundhouse and creative solutions. There was a white sign that said Simple Minds February 15. This intrigued me. This was the band from my generation whose hit "Don't you forget about me" became a huge hit and played in the movie *The Breakfast Club*. I asked about tickets, but also was curious about the creative solutions part of the organization. I mentioned to the attendant Louisa, with long dark hair and what sounded like a North American accent, that I am a writer and told her about me book *Just Keep Going Man*. I described the relevance of the title and that I met a stranger when I got stranded up the Irish causeway and he told me to "just keep going man." Her eyes opened up wide and I could see the whites of them. She said we can do your book launch and handed me a business card. I left the building and got on the tube at Chalk Farm with tears in my eyes. I must have given out 70 business cards in one month to Londoners of all walks of life in the past month, but someone finally took notice. I have rediscovered London and it discovered me.

Private Art Viewing with a Friend

I woke up as usual. Too early. 4:30 am. My wife noticed that my social media account was active and sent me a message. "I see that you're up." Yes I am, and foolishly, I said call me. I was sitting on the brown leather sofa in the back of my building. Kind of an informal business area that also had a public computer. With big glass windows, that when the sun shines through is a very calm feeling and it is a pleasant area to relax, in a very busy part of London that has a main four way street in front of the building. However, really I should have been going back to bed. We did a video phone call on social media and she was in her office chair and during the conversation she tends to lean back instead of forward when I speak to her. It's her way of keeping calm. However, when I mentioned that my first book *Just keep Going Man, a nine city UK tour*, was finished her eyes became wide and she leaned forward with jubilance. I on the other hand was tired and disgruntled with my publisher in the United States. Amidst my move back to the UK, he had sent me eighteen emails and usually the same standard one "any updates yet." I mentioned to him in the fifth or sixth email sent and that I returned, that I have just moved continents, was busy, and overwhelmed but, he did not care. The emails kept coming. I mentioned in my conversation to my wife that a friend of mine thought that I should fire them. I was just about ready too. So, I started my day at 4:30 am, stressed and with negative feelings. I had stamina and energy but the phone call took something out of me. Wind. After our conversation I worked on a few emails and social media communication I had to catch up with.

After a couple of hours, around 9:30am, I went to my health check at the Pimlico Marvin. It took about thirty minutes, I had my blood pressure checked, weight, and had blood taken for just about everything. Everything was generally ok. In the meantime, I would still live. I then went back to my flat. I made a cup of tea and physically and mentally regrouped. Penguin books is near the Panoramic, and being a neophyte at the book writing and publishing business, I thought I might try to get an appointment to see if they would publish my book. I even saw the manager Esme in the lobby of the building and told her that I was going to give it a try, but when I talked to the receptionist at Penguin, they would not even consider talking to me without an agent. I went back to my flat slightly disappointed, but not too surprised. Although now it was 3pm and I had been up already for 11 hours. I checked my email and there was a generic type email from the publisher saying that if my book was not complete with interior and exterior cover by a certain date that I would not receive the money back that I had paid to have it published. The message said that I could receive a refund if I wanted to discontinue working with them, by a certain date. It should not be difficult to figure out what I did next. I replied and requested a refund. I then went upstairs and tried to lay down. I was exhausted. There was another business message from the United States, I now felt my self-going mentally down even further. I tried to relax and watch some "telly." I watched a program about worst next door neighbors. It had a segment about London's most expensive neighborhood Chelsea and Kensington. There are homes as costly as fifty five million pounds in this neighborhood. I thought to myself if one owns a home for a couple of million pounds in London that they are just another number. Confidence is essential to survive in London, but so is humility. If one owns a flat for a million or two pounds, it's really nothing special. There are many amongst you. Humility is essential. Treat everyone with respect.

I finally fell asleep at 9pm but then got up at midnight. I stayed up until 4am, slept for a couple of hours and at about 6am, went downstairs in my building to talk to a friend. I confided in him and told him what happened. He offered to make me tea and I accepted. He had this unique habit of washing the tea bag to which made the tea taste much fresher, which after sitting down and having a sip. It did taste better. However, the conversation got intense, maybe too quickly. He mentioned that his father died before he was born.

He said something like, "why father did you leave me?" I thought of my own son and I immediately broke down in tears, but managed to compose myself. I spoke in polite etiquette and said I told him, "how I deeply sorry I was." I got up and stood across from him. I changed the conversation and shared what I watched on television and how confidence and humility is essential for any Londoner to survive. He shared some stories of when he worked in a hotel and I finished my tea and was about to excuse myself.

"He said come with me, I have to deliver something." We went to the top of my building. Once we got to the top floor, the lift opened up and I was not sure exactly where this was going?

We stood in the lift and he said you see that painting on the wall. It was a modern art painting with thin brush strokes. Kind of like one sees in movies, typifying modern art. "It's worth as much as a London flat." I did not really know what to say. When it came for to me getting off on my floor, he looked at me and said,

"I have a feeling it's going to be a great day," and smiled.

I will never know why he showed me the painting? Was it so I could trust him? And tell him when I was upset or down? Or was it just to reiterate my point about being in London with such wealth nobody is better than anybody, or, maybe he did it just to uplift my mood. I will never know why. Although I know, it was a private viewing of a painting with a friend.

Warm Welcome to Gatwick

I had just arrived back to London, Gatwick airport from Alicante Spain, It was my first trip to Spain, like many people do in the UK, I booked my holiday well in advance to get the best price. And Alicante it was. The trip came at the right time, my book Just Keep Going Man just had been released and I was tired and as an independent publisher, I had been promoting the book on social media myself my first two days in Alicante. Mostly staying up burning the midnight oil. Being a neophyte I did most of the work myself to put my book together, and the process had been an emasculating one, but once it was finished as any author will tell you, it's a great feeling and I had a sense of relief. I also, however, did enjoy Alicante, a city surrounded by brownish mountains with Palm trees. It reminded me of several places I had lived or visited in my life: The Palm trees on the sidewalk that had market stalls selling everything from souvenirs to leather goods, and jewelry. The large sidewalk next to the marina gave a nuance and a cool feel of Florida. An American state that I visited many times when I grew up in Michigan in the USA. The mountainous region took my memory back to when I lived in Erzurum, Turkey. It borders the country of Georgia and I spent one year there from 2010 to 2011. I did manage to see a few of the main attractions, The Santa Barbara Castle: a castle that rests on top of a hill, I had to climb several sets of stairs to go up it and stop to catch my breath a few times, with ten feet high walls and passage ways that a car could pass through. There are old style 17th Century castles cannons that children play on, uninhabited, as children should be. There are no security guards and the ticket entrance office is closed as patrons walk freely. The castle has spectacular views of the city. On day three, I walked past the castle and went to the bull-fighting museum. It was empty and free of charge. On my last day I went to the St. Nicholas cathedral and the contemporary art museum. The St. Nicholas Cathedral has a spectacular dome shaped interior.

I did manage one day to get out of the city and go to Villa Jois. I had however, come to Alicante with a mindset of the pampered tourist and asked the front desk clerk and the tourist information desk about guided tours. The lady who I asked at tourist information seemed agitated by this question and with slight wrinkles and dark bags under her eyes looked like she needed a good night sleep or a break in life. She gave me a timetable for a tram, we have these in Britain, and I am utterly useless at understanding them. I prefer to ask somebody, so that is what I did. I went to the tram station just adjacent next to the train station and asked the tram attendant, who also seemed like he could use a good night sleep or a day off. I tried to be polite as possible. He said to go to Villa Jois and it would cost 4.80 Euros. I tried to pay but my wallet was stuck in the side of my blue pea coat, so I had a hard time pulling it out and just let the people behind go ahead of me. The lady behind me seemed bemused by my manners, but carried on ahead. I managed to pull my wallet out and the attendant was also surprised at my calm courtesy.

It's strange now at just a couple of months before my forty ninth birthday, I have all time in the world, I never rush in cues, or on the stairs in tubes, and the only thing I rush is my work. Alone now with little support from family or friends. There is a maturity of no sense of urgency, but a hardness that the only relationship I believe in is my mother who brought me into this world.

Anyways, the attendant who sold me the ticket told me, "Line one downstairs." I walked away. He repeated. "Line one." When I got downstairs on the tram track, things became easier to understand. There were pictures on the subway of the place or town to go to, and on top of the billboard pics to which line to take. Now I understood. The tram pulled up that said "line one" in bright white on a vertical sign in front of the tram drove along the coast it started to get warmer. The blue sea appeared and sent good vibrations my way, which I needed. When I got to Villa Jois, I walked around and found my way down to the seaside. There were several restaurants at the back of beach, with chairs and tables outside. I picked the one with a decent menu and that was not too crowded, my usual habit so I can read or write on my tablet. I ordered a set menu, which came with a choice of Salad, Main and drink. Tuna Nicosia Salad, Pasta, and a glass of beer. I soaked up the sun, and I read F. Scott Fitzgerald's, *Tender is the Night*. I heard a few English accents in the background. I read and ate my meal.

It was pleasant environment, and I asked for my check and being such an early riser, already around 3pm. I was tired. The next day was my final day so I went to the contemporary art museum, and St Nicholas Cathedral. Both were down side streets, and here I was in another backwoods just like last year when I was up the Irish causeway. It gave me that feeling of adventure, freedom, anything and everything that means anything to me. After I visited a few of these sites, of all places to eat, I ate at Taco Bell that was on one of the main streets. Now I culturally swung back to my American roots, as Taco Bell is a Mexican food and one of the biggest fast food restaurants in the United States. After my lunch, I went back to my hotel and packed, and just set my mind to leaving Alicante. I enjoyed the city, it may not have had the hustle and bustle of some of the other cities in Spain, but it is quite safe and with my Spanish quite rusty since I left the Dominican Republic 11 years ago. Local sellers knew I was a tourist but were honest and considerate. So it was off at 5pm for 9:30pm flight back to London Gatwick.

Always good to arrive back home to the UK with rapid and polite passport control. I took just a backpack but bought another one in a shop that sold goods from Nepal, with multiple colored patterns the backpack looks like something out of the 1960s. It did not take long for my checked bag to come off the conveyer belt. However, by now it was 11:30, I had looked up Gatwick express in Alicante and it operated until 2am but when I arrived at the train station it was closed. I asked an attendant if there were any trains to Victoria and he abruptly said no, the closest you will get is to Blackfriars, an area of London that I am not familiar with. So I thought I would just stay the night in an airport hotel and leave the airport in the morning. First, I checked the Airport Hilton, "sorry sir, we have "no availability," then another small hotel, "sorry we have no vacancies." The attendant said why not try the bloc hotel, so I did but they were full also, so I went back and sat on some seats upstairs and above there was a sign that said, "a warm welcome to Gatwick." I thought that for the first time in my pampered and privileged life I might have to sleep at the airport. Next to me was a man in black jeans with a chain wallet, with a hoodie and he was snoring quite loud. Then on the other side of me was a man with a crew cut perpetually looking at his phone, there was a construction worker in a yellow reflective jacket on standing by the door and it opened every few minutes, and I felt a cold draft. Again, I looked up at the sign a "Warm Welcome to Gatwick." I thought I would check about cabs so I did. The attendant asked for my postcode so I gave it to him.

"That will be exactly 100 pounds sir." I went and withdrew the hundred pounds, but then thought I am a lifelong Londoner and I am not paying this amount of ridiculous money for a cab.

So I went and sat back down next to the guy with the chain wallet. I thought I might give it a try and sleep at the airport. I sat across from the sign again that said "Warm Welcome to Gatwick". The guy with the chain wallet was still there and still snoring. The guy with the crewcut was also still sitting there and staring at his phone still. I tried to join them but started to feel pain siting in an uncomfortable seat, so I caved quickly and went back to the train station. After looking at the departure times I noticed there were two trains left, one at 1:15am to Bedford. On the departure screen it said that it stopped at Kings Cross, I double-checked with the young and tired attendant. He said, "Yep it does." So I went downstairs to the platform and waited for the train. There were hardly any passengers waiting for the train at this time as to be expected. There were two very thin young people, who looked like teenagers also standing for the train. Dressed casually. The boy had on bright blue jogging slacks and trainers (tennis shoes) and the girl with him a faded dark brown pea coat, and also wearing trainers. I figured they must be students. They asked me if the train went to Blackfriars, and I looked at the square box above on the platform that listed train stops, and said yes. The young girl mentioned also that they were going to catch the Gatwick Express, and since it was closed left her scrambling around checking her phone looking for trains to Blackfriars. We started a conversation and they both were from Norway. During the conversation, I mentioned that one is just meant to fend for themselves at this time with public transportation, particularly at this time of the day. There was a teenage girl siting on a bench waiting also for the train and what looked like her father standing next to her. So the total customers for the train was five. After the little girl heard what I said she shouted out,

"We came here with no papers." "I said no papers?" Who must have been her father who was standing behind her, mentioned they were from Iran and only permitted to travel to countries such as Turkey. I went ahead and directly asked "if they were asylum seekers." "Yes," the father replied. Now my journey was getting interesting. The train arrives and the little girl and her father sit in the same empty carriage, but away from me while the two Norwegian teenagers sit next to me. We talk about how there are CCTV Cameras all over London, my book, and how Norway is a very affluent country, but very cold in the winter. They get off at Blackfriars and I sit alone on the empty train to Kings Cross. There is one more stop before then and I hear a slam of the door and see a passenger mumbling to himself. I sit not being afraid, but as soon as the train stops for Kings Cross I make a mad dash for the exits and St Pancras station to the Taxi stand. By this time it was about 3am. I tell the taxi driver I live at 152 Grosvenor Road, but he is not familiar with it so I mention it's just near Vauxhall Bridge. I arrive at the building around 3:30am, pay the driver and then ring the buzzer just outside the revolving glass doorway and wake up the concierge. I go up to my flat on the fifth floor, walk in to a cold flat turn the heat on, which has been blowing too hot for some time now and climb into my bed. I feel the burst of heat touch my toes. I now got my warm welcome.

Dusk at Pimlico, the End

Two of the staff said, "It's the end of an era," that I was leaving the Panoramic. They could have been just being polite, maybe, but life is sometimes about letting go. This is my last view of dusk at Pimlico.

Figure 1 Picture of the River Thames in Pimlico

Figure 2 Picture from my flat, its Dusk at Pimlico.

Figure 3 Picture of my grandparents with my Auntie Jean who just passed away March 2018

Figure 4 Picture from the Bull Fighting Museum in Alicante

Figure 5 Inside St. Nicholas Cathedral in Alicante

Made in the USA
Lexington, KY
11 May 2018